SECOND EDITION

TOUCHSTONE

WORKBOOK 4A

MICHAEL MCCARTHY
JEANNE MCCARTEN
HELEN SANDIFORD

CAMBRIDGE
UNIVERSITY PRESS & ASSESSMENT

Shaftesbury Road, Cambridge CB2 8EA, United Kingdom

One Liberty Plaza, 20th Floor, New York, NY 10006, USA

477 Williamstown Road, Port Melbourne, VIC 3207, Australia

314–321, 3rd Floor, Plot 3, Splendor Forum, Jasola District Centre, New Delhi – 110025, India

103 Penang Road, #05-06/07, Visioncrest Commercial, Singapore 238467

Cambridge University Press & Assessment is a department of the University of Cambridge.

We share the University's mission to contribute to society through the pursuit of education, learning and research at the highest international levels of excellence.

www.cambridge.org
Information on this title: www.cambridge.org/9781107627086

© Cambridge University Press & Assessment 2005, 2014

This publication is in copyright. Subject to statutory exception and to the provisions of relevant collective licensing agreements, no reproduction of any part may take place without the written permission of Cambridge University Press & Assessment.

First published 2005
Second Edition 2014

20 19 18 17 16 15 14 13 12 11

Printed in Great Britain by Ashford Colour Press Ltd.

A catalog record for this publication is available from the British Library.

ISBN 978-1-107-68043-2 Student's Book
ISBN 978-1-107-62430-6 Student's Book A
ISBN 978-1-107-63748-1 Student's Book B
ISBN 978-1-107-68275-7 Workbook
ISBN 978-1-107-62708-6 Workbook A
ISBN 978-1-107-69602-0 Workbook B
ISBN 978-1-107-66153-2 Full Contact
ISBN 978-1-107-67936-8 Full Contact A
ISBN 978-1-107-66763-1 Full Contact B
ISBN 978-1-107-68151-4 Teacher's Edition with Assessment Audio CD/CD-ROM
ISBN 978-1-107-61272-3 Class Audio CDs (4)

Additional resources for this publication at www.cambridge.org/touchstone2

Cambridge University Press & Assessment has no responsibility for the persistence or accuracy of URLs for external or third-party internet websites referred to in this publication, and does not guarantee that any content on such websites is, or will remain, accurate or appropriate. Information regarding prices, travel timetables, and other factual information given in this work is correct at the time of first printing but Cambridge University Press & Assessment does not guarantee the accuracy of such information thereafter.

Contents

1 Interesting lives 2
2 Personal tastes 10
3 World cultures 18
4 Socializing 26
5 Law and order 34
6 Strange events 42

Interesting lives

UNIT 1

Lesson A Interviews

1 Meet Alex. . . .

Grammar **Claire is interviewing Alex, a successful photographer, for a news website. Circle the correct verb forms to complete the conversation.**

Claire When **did you start** / **were you starting** taking photos?

Alex Gosh, **I'm taking** / **I've been taking** photos since I was about six.

Claire Really? So, what kind of camera **did you use** / **have you used** back then?

Alex Well, when I was young, my uncle **showed** / **was showing** me how to use this old camera and how to develop the prints. I still use it!

Claire That's amazing. So, what projects **do you work** / **are you working** on currently?

Alex I just started this nature series. **I'm taking** / **I was taking** photos of trees. You know, trees that have interesting shapes.

Claire That's great. How many tree photos **have you taken** / **have you been taking** so far?

Alex A lot. Hundreds.

Claire Really? And how has your work changed? I mean, what kind of photography **were you doing** / **have you been doing** five years ago?

Alex Well, I **was working** / **'ve worked** on some color portraits for a competition. I **didn't win** / **wasn't winning**, but it was a good experience.

2 About you 1

Grammar **Write the questions using a correct verb form. Then write true answers.**

1. What / you take / photos of lately ? *What have you been taking photos of lately?*
   I've been taking photos of my friends and interesting buildings in my hometown.
2. How long / you / have / a camera ? _____
   _____
3. your parents / take / many photos of you when you were a child ? _____
   _____
4. you ever / be / to a photographer's studio ? _____
   _____
5. When / you last take a photo ? _____
   _____
6. What / social networking sites / you / post / your photos on currently ? _____
   _____

3 Questions and answers

Grammar **Complete each conversation with the correct form of the verb given. Sometimes more than one answer is possible.**

1. (watch)

Ben What kinds of movies ___*have*___ you ___*been watching*___ lately?

Kumi Well, mostly I _____ horror movies. I usually _____ three or four horror movies a month. Actually, I _____ a great horror movie last night.

2. (live)

Ana _____ you ever _____ in another country?

Joel Yes, I _____ in two other countries. I _____ in Canada for three years after I left college, and I _____ in Kenya until last June.

3. (eat)

Christa You look great. What's your secret?

Jalila Thanks. I _____ a lot of vegetables and whole grains lately. And I always _____ six small meals a day. I just _____ a salad for lunch.

4. (write)

Vito How long _____ you _____ poetry?

Kim Um. I guess I _____ poetry for about four years. I _____ almost every day if I can. Yesterday, I _____ for almost three hours nonstop!

4 About you 2

Grammar **Answer the questions with true information.**

1. How long have you been studying English? ___*I've been studying English for five years.*___
2. Have you ever lived in another country? _____
3. What kinds of music are you listening to these days? _____
4. What kinds of TV shows do you watch? _____
5. What did you do during your last vacation? _____
6. What were you doing at this time last week? _____

It's a long story!

1 Dream jobs

Grammar and vocabulary

Circle the correct words to complete the paragraphs.

1. LEIGH HUDSON tells us how she seemed / ended up / decided being an editor.

Well, after I **imagined / finished / bothered** taking my law school entrance exams, I still wasn't sure if I wanted to be a lawyer. I already had a degree in English and was **considering / expecting / agreeing** training to be a journalist. Then one day, I saw an ad for an editorial assistant on a publishing company's website, and I **offered / expected / decided** to apply for it. After the interview, the manager said I was right for the job and **offered / ended up / considered** to pay me a good salary. I immediately **agreed / finished / missed** to take the job. Anyway, I've been working at the company for over five years, and now I'm a senior editor. I absolutely love my job – I can't **agree / expect / imagine** doing anything else!

2. GEORGE ALLEN explains how he became a chef.

I wasn't really **agreeing / missing / planning on** being a chef. I **spent / bothered / decided** four years in college studying electrical engineering. After I graduated, I **agreed / happened / started** working at an engineering firm and had a great salary, but a lot of responsibility. After six months, I **intend / remember / miss** thinking, "Am I really happy being an electrical engineer?" I decided I wasn't happy at all, so I quit my job and applied to a local cooking school. After I finished training, I opened a small restaurant. I've never **ended up / missed / offered** working at my old job – not once. And that was 15 years ago now!

3. CELIA MENDEZ tells us how she became a dancer.

Well, a few years ago, my friends and I **happened / seemed / missed** to go on vacation to a Caribbean resort that put on a great show every night with singing and dancing and everything. I was taking dance classes at the time, and I was actually **finishing / bothering / considering** becoming a dancer. Anyway, one night, the resort had a talent competition for the guests. I didn't **imagine / happen / bother** to sign up. But my friends said, "Celia, this **seems / spends / expects** to be a perfect opportunity for you. You're such a good dancer. You should do it!" Well, to make a long story short, I won the talent competition, and the resort offered me a position as a dancer! I never **happened / expected / ended up** to be a successful professional dancer, least of all at a Caribbean resort! Dreams really do come true!

2 How I ended up living in New York City

Grammar and vocabulary **Complete the paragraph with the correct form of the verbs.**

A lot of people ask me how I ended up *living* (live) in New York City. Well, actually, I wasn't planning on _____ (be) here. It's just that the opportunity came up when my friend Samuela happened _____ (move) here for college. She needed a roommate, so I agreed _____ (share) an apartment with her in the city. We were only in the apartment a couple of months when Samuela started _____ (miss) home. She said she missed _____ (be) with her family. I guess she couldn't imagine _____ (stay) three more years and _____ (be) happy. So, she decided _____ (complete) the semester, and then she transferred to a college back home. Anyway, I kept the apartment and found a great job. I've been here for over six years now, but Samuela and I are still great friends. We've never stopped _____ (email) each other, and we call each other all the time. We just live in different cities – that's all!

3 About you

Grammar and vocabulary **Answer the questions with true information.**

1. Where do you think you'll end up living in a few years?
   I think I'll end up living in Paris after I finish school.
2. What are you planning on doing when you finish this English course?
   _____
3. Have you started reading a new book recently?
   _____
4. What's something fun you remember doing as a child?
   _____
5. Have you ever decided to do something and then regretted it?
   _____
6. Do you expect to get a good grade in this class?
   _____
7. What do you intend to do this weekend?
   _____
8. Is there anything you can't imagine doing in life?
   _____

Lesson C We're both getting scared. . . .

1 When I was little, . . .

Conversation strategies **Read the conversation. Change the underlined verbs to the simple present to highlight the key moments.**

Freda This pie reminds me of the time my sister made me eat a mud pie.

Chris You're kidding! What happened?

Freda Well, when I was very little, she and I used to play together, and we would always play outside, you know?

Chris Yeah. We always played outside, too. Not like kids nowadays.

Freda Well, anyway, one day, I was (*'m / am*) in the yard, and she made me eat a mud pie. Here she was, seven years old, in the yard with three beautiful mud pies. She said, "Freda, try this. It's so good." And she acted like she put some in her mouth. I was three years old, so what did I know?

Chris Oh, no! What did it taste like?

Freda I don't remember.

Chris Really?

Freda No. But I remember being sick afterward.

2 I'll never forget . . .

Conversation strategies **Read the conversation. Change some verbs in Sarah's story to the simple present or present continuous to highlight key moments in the story.**

Sarah Did I ever tell you about the time I ran out of cash in South Korea?

Lisa No. What happened?

Sarah Well, I was traveling through South Korea, way out in the middle of nowhere, and I ~~ran out~~ (*run out*) of cash and I had no way of getting back to Seoul.

Lisa Really? You didn't have any traveler's checks or anything?

Sarah Well, I had one check for 50 dollars, but I was in the mountains, and there was nowhere to exchange it.

Lisa Oh, no! So, what did you do?

Sarah Well, I was getting pretty nervous. I was walking around and couldn't find a bank or anything. Anyway, finally, I met this really nice French man. So I explained the situation, and he agreed to take my traveler's check in exchange for Korean money. So at least I had enough money to get a bus to the nearest town. And so yeah, I went to the most expensive hotel.

Lisa Why the most expensive hotel?

Sarah Well, back then, small hotels didn't accept credit cards. And it was a holiday, so the banks were closed.

Lisa So you stayed there?

Sarah Yeah. I ended up booking a room for the night, and then the next day, I found a bank and got some cash. So it all worked out in the end.

3 This great bike path

Conversation strategies **Complete the story with *this* or *these*.**

My friends went bike riding one day on ___this___ great bike path in the country. The bike path is really _____ old railroad track that isn't used by trains anymore. Anyway, it goes through all _____ beautiful old farms. But, you see, my friends are from the city, so they're not used to seeing farm animals and fields and stuff. So, my friends are riding along, and they see all _____ goats in a field. Well, they stop to take photos, but they have no idea that goats can be a little unfriendly. Suddenly, they see _____ big goat running toward them, so they jump back on their bikes and ride away, you know, really quickly. Then _____ guy starts yelling at them. It turns out it's the farmer, and they're riding their bikes on his field.

4 Really?

Conversation strategies **Rewrite these stories. Use the simple present or present continuous to highlight some key moments in each story. Use *this* and *these* to highlight important people, things, or events.**

1. You know, a friend of mine is always seeing famous people when she's out. One time, she was checking out a computer in a computer store. And all of a sudden, she looked up and saw her favorite basketball player. He was standing next to her – checking out the same computer!
   You know, this friend of mine is always seeing famous people when she's out. One time, she was checking out this computer in a computer store. And all of a sudden, . . .

2. You know, my cousin Adam met his fiancée because of his dog. He has an enormous dog named Scruffy. Well, one day they were in the park. Anyway, Scruffy started chasing a squirrel and pulled my cousin right into a woman. So, Adam apologized, and he and the woman started talking. And to make a long story short, now they're engaged!
   _____
   _____
   _____

3. I remember one time my friend Linda had a party. It was for her graduation, I think, and we were all outdoors. Anyway, the weather was beautiful at first, but after an hour or so, some dark clouds started coming in, and it started to rain really hard. So, she just turned on a radio, and we all started dancing in the rain. We had so much fun. It was the best party ever.
   _____
   _____
   _____

1 Super man

Reading **A Read the article. What do you think an *activist* is?**

- ☐ a successful actor
- ☐ someone who is physically active
- ☐ a motivational speaker
- ☐ someone who works for a cause

Inspiring in Life and Death

Until 1995, Christopher Reeve was living a life most people only dream about. He was a successful actor – famous for his roles in the *Superman* movies – and happily married with three children. He had everything to live for.

Then on May 27, 1995, his life changed dramatically. Reeve fell off his horse while riding in a horse-jumping competition. The accident left him with serious injuries – a fracture in the second vertebra of his neck – and Reeve was left paralyzed from his neck down.

Reeve was confined to a wheelchair and had to depend on his wife, nurses, doctors, and therapists to do everything for him. He could no longer walk, hold anything in his hands, or feed or wash himself. He also relied on a respirator to help him breathe.

Many people may have given up hope and felt sorry for themselves. But not Christopher Reeve.

Shortly after his accident, Reeve said, "The only limits you have are the ones you put on yourself." With this positive attitude, he began adjusting to his new life.

Amazingly, he continued to act in movies and direct them. But most importantly, he became an activist for people with spinal cord injuries. He raised money for research and started the Christopher & Dana Reeve Foundation, which awards money to people researching cures for paralysis. He wrote an autobiography, *Still Me*. He even testified before the U.S. Senate to encourage funding for stem-cell research.

Although Reeve never recovered from his injuries, he remained hopeful throughout his life about finding a cure for paralysis. By not giving up hope, he gave other people with disabilities hope that in the future, recovery won't be against all odds.

Christopher Reeve
September 25, 1952–October 10, 2004

B Read the article again. Then answer the questions.

1. What movies did Christopher Reeve star in? _____
2. What was Reeve doing when he hurt his neck? _____
3. Who did Reeve have to rely on for help? _____
4. What does the Christopher & Dana Reeve Foundation do? _____

_____

2 How I overcame stage fright

Writing **A Read the anecdote. Then put the story in the correct order by writing each number in the correct box.**

1. Set the general time or place.
2. Set the particular time or place.
3. Describe what happened.
4. End the story. Link the events to now.

☐ So, with that memory in my mind, I calmed down and walked on stage. I looked at the audience, and I thought, "I know you want me to do well." I closed my eyes and played a great recital.

☐ Today, remembering my teacher's words helps me to be confident when I perform. And it helps me with a lot of other things, too!

☐ I'm a musician, and when I was in graduate school, I had to give a final violin recital to get my degree. I was nervous because there were so many talented students at my school.

☐ On the night of the recital, I was so nervous that my hands were shaking. But I remembered what my very first teacher said to me years before: "People are here because they want you to do well."

B Use the steps above to write an anecdote about something you were nervous about doing and how you overcame it.

Unit 1 Progress chart

	What can you do? Mark the boxes. ✓ = I can . . . ? = I need to review how to . . .	To review, go back to these pages in the Student's Book.
Grammar	☐ use the simple and continuous forms of verbs. ☐ use verbs that are followed by verb + *-ing* or *to* + verb.	2 and 3 4 and 5
Vocabulary	☐ use at least 10 new verbs.	2, 4, and 5
Conversation strategies	☐ use the present tense to highlight key moments in a story. ☐ use *this* and *these* to highlight key people, things, and events.	6 7
Writing	☐ write an anecdote.	9

Personal tastes

UNIT 2

Lesson A Makeovers

1 Confessions of a fashion queen

Grammar and vocabulary **Complete the sentences with the words in the box.**

hard important much nice ✓often quickly

1. I go shopping as *often* as I can. I go almost every other day.
2. You can't look your best if you get ready as _____ as possible. It's better to take your time.
3. Jeans can look just as _____ as pants if you wear them with a cool top.
4. For me, comfort isn't as _____ as style when it comes to choosing clothes.
5. I try as _____ as I can to look great every day. I pay a lot of attention to how I look.
6. I don't like bright colors as _____ as dark colors. I almost always wear black.

2 Dear Vera, . . .

Grammar and vocabulary **Complete the letters with the words and expressions in the box.**

fast ✓interested in fashion little time many things much attention scruffy

❶ Dear Vera,

My boyfriend isn't as *interested in fashion* as I am, and he wears the same clothes all the time. He really needs a makeover. How can I help him look better? – *JB, Vancouver*

Dear JB,

Lots of people don't pay as _____ to their appearance as their partners would like. Gently let your boyfriend know that you want to help him look better. Help him pick out clothes that aren't as _____ as the ones he wears now. Your boyfriend might not want your help at first, but he'll be glad when people start noticing how good he looks. – *Vera*

❷ Dear Vera,

It takes me so long to get ready in the morning, and I always end up being late for work. I need to get ready as _____ as possible. What should I do? – *CN, Taipei*

Dear CN,

Mornings are always difficult. You need to spend as _____ as possible organizing yourself. So, to save time, do as _____ as you can the night before. Pick out your clothes before you go to bed, and put everything you need for the day in your bag. That way, your mornings won't be as rushed. – *Vera*

3 She isn't as . . .

Grammar and vocabulary

Look at the pictures of Sachi and Nell. How are they alike or different? Write sentences with *as . . . as* or *not as . . . as*.

1. (tall) *Sachi isn't as tall as Nell.*
2. (hair / short) _____
3. (many dark clothes) _____
4. (skirt / long) _____
5. (shoes / comfortable) _____
6. (much jewelry) _____
7. (earrings / big) _____
8. They both love fashion. (interested in fashion) _____

4 About you

Grammar and vocabulary

Answer the questions with true information. Use *as . . . as* or *not as . . . as*.

1. Do you generally wear bright colors as often as dark colors?
   I don't wear bright colors as often as dark colors. I'm most comfortable in black.
2. Do you spend as much money on clothes as your friends?
   _____
3. Do you try as hard as you can to be trendy and fashionable?
   _____
4. Do you have as many accessories as your best friend?
   _____
5. Do your parents care as much about their appearance as you do?
   _____
6. Do you find stylish clothes to be as comfortable as casual clothes?
   _____
7. Do you spend as little time as possible getting ready in the morning?
   _____

1 Isn't that dress awful?

Grammar **Complete the conversations with *isn't, aren't, don't,* or *doesn't*.**

1. A Oh, look at that dress. *Isn't* it awful?
   B Oh, I don't know. It's what's in style. _____ you interested in fashion?
   A Not really. Are you?
   B Kind of. But look at this dress. _____ it have something special about it?
   A Yeah, it has something all right – a $5,000 price tag! _____ that a little expensive for a dress?
   B Yeah. But being fashionable isn't cheap.

2. A Are you ready yet?
   B Yes, almost. I . . . um . . . just need to find a tie.
   A _____ you have lots of ties?
   B Yeah, but they're all dirty.
   A You should wear a jacket, too, _____ you think?
   B But it's warm outside. _____ this outfit look good?
   A Well, . . . um, _____ your socks different colors?
   B Oh, yeah. You're right. I need to find socks now, too!

2 Don't you think . . . ?

Grammar **Rewrite the sentences as negative questions.**

1. Leather jackets are cool.
   Aren't leather jackets cool?
2. Most sneakers cost way too much nowadays.
   _____
3. A tie is a great way to complete a man's outfit.
   _____
4. Plaid looks great with floral prints.
   _____
5. It's hard to find jeans that fit well.
   _____
6. Neon green and orange are great colors.
   _____

3 What's in fashion?

Vocabulary **A** **Look at the picture and read the comments. Two things in each description are wrong. Underline the wrong word(s) and correct the sentences.**

1. Luis looks very stylish in his denim jeans and a short-sleeved shirt. His neon striped tie looks cool, too.
   Luis looks very stylish in his denim jeans and a long-sleeved shirt.
   His polka-dot tie looks cool, too.

2. Kate looks great in that plaid silk skirt. Her cashmere turtleneck sweater goes with it really well, too.
   _____
   _____

3. Tiana's wearing dark blue skinny jeans – as usual – with a leather jacket. That look never goes out of fashion.
   _____
   _____

4. Ravi's light gray scarf goes perfectly with his suede jacket. Those fitted casual pants look great, too.
   _____
   _____

B **Look at the pictures. Write descriptions of Angelo's and Risa's clothing.**

1. Angelo _____
   _____
   _____

2. Risa _____
   _____
   _____

She has a big collection, then.

1 So, you must like . . .

Conversation strategies **Circle the response that best summarizes what A says.**

1. A I like music that's calm – music that helps me unwind after a crazy day.
   a. So, you have broad tastes, then.
   b. Uh-huh. You like music that's relaxing.
2. A I love Passion Pit. I've seen them in concert five times, and I have all their albums.
   a. So, you're a big fan.
   b. You like a lot of bands, then.
3. A I have a laptop, a smartphone, a tablet, and an e-reader.
   a. You don't know much about electronics.
   b. So, you have every gadget you need.
4. A I don't like the school cafeteria. They have the same things on the menu day after day.
   a. Yeah. I don't like it, either.
   b. Yeah. There's not much variety.

2 Summing it up

Conversation strategies **Complete the conversation with the sentences in the box.**

✓You have definite tastes, then.	You like songs that you know the lyrics to.
You like clothes that you can wear every day.	You want to understand what you're looking at.

Russ So anyway, you asked me what kind of music I like. Well, I like jazz, but I don't like blues. And I like rock, but I'm not really into pop. I guess I listen mostly to classical music, though not new stuff.

Liza *You have definite tastes, then.*

Russ Yeah. I guess. I just know what I like and what I don't. What about you?

Liza Well, I like music I can dance to – music that makes me feel good. I love it when I can sing along.

Russ I know what you mean. _____

Liza Exactly. I like music that puts me in a good mood.

Russ Yeah, I know what you're saying.

Liza It's the same with art. I like to be able to look at a picture and recognize what it is. Is it a flower or a car? Is it a man or a woman? You know what I mean?

Russ I know. _____

Liza That's right. I don't like art that's too weird.

Russ That's kind of how I feel about fashion. I like all the new fashions, but I'm not sure I'd ever wear them. Some styles are a little too weird for my taste, you know? They're just not practical.

Liza Right. _____

Russ Yes. I'm just conservative, I guess.

3 Now, what do you like?

Conversation strategies

Add *Now* to the conversation in two appropriate places. Change the capital letters and add commas where necessary.

Avery I guess I'm pretty traditional, you know. I have conservative tastes in most things, like music and fashion.

Mike Really? I guess you don't listen to techno music, right?

Avery No way!

Mike _____ Are you the same about food, too?

Avery Actually, I like trying different foods. _____ I guess I'm not as conservative when it comes to eating.

Mike Interesting! _____ Have you tried sushi?

Avery Yes, I have. _____ And I love it!

4 Now, is there . . . ?

Conversation strategies

Read Kay's comments about her likes and dislikes. Use the cues to complete each conversation with a summarizing response and a follow-up question with *Now*.

1. Kay I listen to all kinds of music – jazz, classical, hip-hop, rock.
   You (you / have / pretty broad tastes in music) *So, you have pretty broad tastes in music.*
   Kay Yeah, I guess I do!
   You (you / have a favorite) *Now, do you have a favorite?*
   Kay No, I pretty much like everything!

2. Kay Isn't this weather terrible? It's been over 90 degrees for at least eight days in a row! I can't stand it.
   You (you / not like / hot weather) _____
   Kay No, I don't like hot weather at all.
   You (you / like / cold weather) _____
   Kay Absolutely! I'm a skier, so I love cold weather.

3. Kay My car is really old, so I always worry that it's going to break down. I never know if it's going to start or not.
   You (it / be / pretty unreliable) _____
   Kay Yeah, it is. Maybe I need a new one.
   You (what kind of car / you / like) _____
   Kay I'm not really sure. Anything, if it's reliable.

Lesson D Personal style

1 Street fashion

Reading **A Read the interviews.**

Which person is the most interested in fashion? _____

Who is the least interested? _____

How would you describe your style?

My style? It's casual and easy. I wear things that aren't too fussy – things that are comfortable and easy to wear. It's a little plain, but not too plain – I always wear a little color.

What does your style say about you?

My style says I'm easygoing. I like to look good, but I'm not going to spend a lot of time in front of the mirror. It says you should try to get to know me in a deeper way than just looking at the outside. There are other things more important than clothes.

How do you express yourself through the clothes you wear?

I don't, really. I don't spend a lot of time thinking about my clothes. I'd rather express myself in other ways, like talking to people or writing.

Sadie

How would you describe your style?

I wear casual but stylish things that don't stand out, or aren't too different. I like my clothes to be simple, but I usually take more of a risk with my shoes.

What does your style say about you?

It reflects my desire to be fashionable, but is not a demand for attention. For example, at parties I usually talk to one person at a time, rather than trying to be really outgoing. I'm more laid-back.

How do you express yourself through the clothes you wear?

My clothes are a way of showing the outside world what to expect. When I go out, people can guess that I'm relaxed and friendly. My clothes make me look approachable.

Carlos

How would you describe your style?

Unique. I mix lots of different styles together to make my individual style. Some days I'll wear a lace skirt with a plaid wool vest and tights in a cool pattern. And sometimes I'll put on a vintage hat to complete the look.

What does your style say about you?

My style says I'm unpredictable. I change from one day to the next. You can't put a particular label on me, like "She's preppy," or "She's classic," or "trendy," or whatever.

How do you express yourself through the clothes you wear?

It's fun to wear things that make people guess about you. People don't know who I am when they see my clothes, because I don't look just like everyone else. I like to be a little mysterious, to keep a few secrets about myself.

Michi

B Find the words below in the interviews and circle the best meaning.

1. fussy	a. simple	b. very detailed or decorated
2. stand out	a. look different	b. look the same
3. a desire	a. something you really want	b. something you don't want
4. approachable	a. easy to talk to	b. unfriendly or shy
5. unpredictable	a. conservative and average	b. strange and difficult to guess

C Read the questions. Check (✓) the names in the chart.

	Sadie	Carlos	Michi
1. Who likes to stand out in a crowd?	☐	☐	☑
2. Who likes to wear comfortable clothes?	☐	☐	☐
3. Who thinks their clothes shouldn't reveal their true personality?	☐	☐	☐
4. Who likes to change their look the most?	☐	☐	☐
5. Who likes to look nice, but not too different?	☐	☐	☐

2 Fashion tips

Writing **A Read the fashion tips and add the appropriate punctuation: commas (,), dashes (–), or exclamation marks (!).**

1. If you want to take care of your clothes you should wash them regularly dry them carefully and store them properly.
2. Choose clothes that make you feel good clothes that reflect your individual style.
3. Buy clothes that you can wear for more than one season that way you will get the most out of your new clothes.
4. Mix classic designs with trendier pieces wear simple black pants with a fun belt a trendy shirt and a classic jacket. You'll never be out of style.

B What is your fashion advice? Write three of your own fashion tips.

Unit 2 Progress chart

	What can you do? Mark the boxes. ✓ = I can . . . ? = I need to review how to . . .	To review, go back to these pages in the Student's Book.
Grammar	☐ make comparisons using *as . . . as* and *not as . . . as*. ☐ ask negative questions when I want someone to agree with me.	12 and 13 14
Vocabulary	☐ use at least 20 new words and expressions to talk about fashion.	12, 13, and 15
Conversation strategies	☐ show understanding by summarizing what someone says. ☐ use *Now* to introduce a follow-up question on a different aspect of a topic.	16 17
Writing	☐ use commas (,), dashes (–), and exclamation marks (!).	19

World cultures

UNIT 3

Lesson A Traditional things

1 Traditions

Grammar **Complete the conversation with the simple present passive.**

Ken What's your favorite tradition from when you were a child?

Kerstin Hmm . . . let's see . . . I'd say Santa Lucia's Day.

Ken Santa Lucia's Day? I've never heard of it. Is it a Swedish festival?

Kerstin Yeah. It *'s celebrated* (celebrate) on December thirteenth. It's the darkest time of winter, and Santa Lucia _____ (consider) to be the symbol of light. So, it reminds everyone that the days will get longer and sunnier after December.

Ken Oh, I see. So what do you do to celebrate?

Kerstin Well, in schools, for example, one girl _____ (choose) to be Santa Lucia. She wears a white dress, and a crown of candles _____ (place) on her head. Then the Santa Lucia song _____ (sing) by everyone. And in some families, the girl serves her parents breakfast in bed. That _____ (not do) in all homes, though.

Ken So, is there a special kind of food that _____ (eat), or anything?

Kerstin Yeah, they have these sweet buns that _____ (make) with spices. They _____ usually _____ (serve) with coffee – or juice for the kids.

Ken Huh. It sounds nice.

2 Did you know?

Grammar **Rewrite each sentence using the simple present passive. Use *by* when the "doer" of the action is given.**

1. Some Native Americans carve totem poles out of wood.
   Totem poles are carved out of wood by some Native Americans.
2. They make the traditional Spanish dish, *paella*, with chicken, seafood, and saffron.
   _____
3. In Mexico, they celebrate the Day of the Dead on the first two days in November.
   _____
4. In Taiwan, parents give children red envelopes with money inside on New Year's Day.
   _____

3 So you want to know about Ireland . . .

Grammar **Complete the web page with the verbs in the boxes. Use the simple present passive.**

About Ireland

ABOUT IRELAND

SPORTS

✓call call hold play use

The Irish love international sports like soccer and rugby, but they have their very own national sports, too. One traditional sport in Ireland *is called* *hurling*. Sticks, or *hurleys*, _____ to hit a ball, a *sliotar*. Matches are usually 70 minutes long and _____ between two teams. Women play a similar sport, which _____ *camogie*. The final match _____ every September in Dublin.

MUSIC

call learn not use perform sing

Music is a strong tradition in Ireland. A typical musical event _____ a "session." Sessions _____ in pubs, clubs, and homes, where musicians and singers get together to play Irish music in an informal setting. Sheet music _____ at a traditional session because the tunes and songs _____ by heart. Some of the oldest songs _____ without musical accompaniment.

FOOD

boil make mash mix serve

One of Ireland's dishes, *colcannon*, _____ traditionally on Halloween. It _____ with potatoes and cabbage, which _____ in separate pots. The potatoes _____ until creamy, and then they _____ with the cabbage, leeks, milk, spices, and butter, and baked in a pan.

4 About you

Grammar **Complete the questions with the verbs in parentheses. Then answer the questions with true information using the simple present passive.**

1. What sport *is considered* (consider) a traditional sport in your country?
   Kite flying is considered a traditional sport in South Korea.
2. What handicrafts _____ typically _____ (make)?
   _____
3. What drinks _____ traditionally _____ (serve)?
   _____
4. What kinds of traditional games _____ (play)?
   _____
5. What special occasions _____ (celebrate)?
   _____
6. What traditional songs _____ (sing)?
   _____

1 Mind your manners!

Grammar and vocabulary **Use the words in the box to complete the sentences with either verb + *-ing* or *to* + verb.**

1. Italy: It's customary *to kiss* friends and family when you meet.
2. South Korea: _____ your bare feet to elderly people is disrespectful.
3. Indonesia: _____ and drinking before you are asked to by your host is rude.
4. The U.S.A.: It's impolite _____ at a bus stop or in a bank, for example.
5. Mexico: _____ is the normal way to greet people in a business situation.
6. Japan: It's important _____ your shoes before you enter someone's home.
7. Saudi Arabia: _____ in public is a sign of friendship.
8. Germany: If you're sitting, it's polite _____ when greeting people and shaking their hands.

cut in line
eat
hold hands
✓kiss
shake hands
show
stand up
take off

2 Manners dos and don'ts

Grammar and vocabulary **Look at the pictures and complete the sentences.**

1. In the United States, you should try *to keep* your voice down in a library.

2. In Japan, _____ is a way of showing respect.

3. _____ an argument in public in Vietnam is considered bad manners.

4. _____ around barefoot in Belize is an acceptable custom.

5. It's acceptable not _____ waiters in Australia, unless you're at a very fancy restaurant.

6. It's bad manners in Indonesia _____ at someone with your finger.

3 Good manners

Grammar **Complete the sentences with the correct form of the verbs. Then check (✓) the sentences that are true in your country. Circle the six most important ones.**

GOOD MANNERS CHECKLIST

1. ____ You can offend people by *reaching* (reach) across a table for something.
2. ____ It's polite _____ (say) hello to your teacher when you arrive in class.
3. ____ _____ (eat) on the subway is considered rude.
4. ____ _____ (be) five minutes late for a meeting is acceptable.
5. ____ It's considered rude _____ (shout) at someone.
6. ____ It's not acceptable _____ (go) to a party uninvited.
7. ____ People are expected _____ (be) on time for medical and dental appointments.
8. ____ Be careful not _____ (leave) work without _____ (say) good night to your co-workers.
9. ____ _____ (give) money for a wedding gift is common.
10. ____ _____ (ask) about someone's age might be offensive.
11. ____ When a train stops, it's better _____ (wait) for people to get off before _____ (get) on yourself.
12. ____ It's bad manners _____ (talk) loudly on a cell phone in public places.

4 About you

Grammar **Rewrite the sentences using *not* to give them an opposite meaning. Then check (✓) the sentences that are true in your country.**

1. ____ It's OK to point at people in public places.
   ____ *It's not OK to point at people in public places.*
2. ____ It's customary to walk in someone's house without taking off your shoes.
   ____ _____
3. ____ Try to stand close to people you're talking to.
   ____ _____
4. ____ Opening a gift in front of the person who gave it to you is considered rude.
   ____ _____
5. ____ You can annoy people by saying you're sorry if you bump into them.
   ____ _____
6. ____ It's customary to tip hairstylists.
   ____ _____
7. ____ Being early for a party is considered polite.
   ____ _____
8. ____ Talking on a cell phone in a public place is acceptable.
   ____ _____

Lesson C To be honest, . . .

1 I really like it.

Conversation strategies **Rewrite each response using the best expression to make the response sound more direct.**

1. A Do you like your new dorm?
   B Yeah. I like it.
   (really / sort of) *I really like it.*

2. A What's your new roommate like?
   B Well, I don't really like her.
   (to be honest / I guess) _____

3. A Do you miss anything about your old school?
   B No. I hated my old school.
   (absolutely / a little bit) _____

4. A Do you ever think about studying abroad?
   B Yes! I would like to do that.
   (kind of / definitely) _____

5. A If you moved away, would you miss your family?
   B Oh, I'd miss my family, especially my brother.
   (in a way / certainly) _____

2 About you 1

Conversation strategies **Rewrite the sentences so that they are true for you. Use different expressions from the box. Add more information.**

absolutely	certainly	honestly	really	to tell you the truth
actually	definitely	in fact	to be honest	

1. I love learning about new cultures.
   I really love learning about new cultures. I'd absolutely love to go to Kenya.

2. I don't think it would be exciting to live in a new city.
   _____

3. I'd miss home cooking if I lived in another country.
   _____

4. I'd hate to live with a roommate. I'd prefer to live by myself.
   _____

5. I'd like to live all over the world. I can't imagine living in just one place.
   _____

6. I'm sure I'd get homesick if I lived a long way from home.
   _____

3 Of course . . .

Conversation strategies **Use *of course* twice in each conversation where it is appropriate and not rude. Leave one blank in each conversation empty. Add commas where necessary.**

1. Bruno I hear you decided to study abroad next year. Where are you going?
   Kara _____ I'm going to Mexico!
   Bruno You must be so excited! I know I would be.
   Kara Yeah, I'm definitely excited, but I'm really nervous, too.
   Bruno Just think about all the cool experiences you'll have.
   Kara Yeah, I know. But I'm going to miss you _____ !
   I mean, who am I going to talk to when I have a problem?
   Bruno Well, *me* _____ . We can always chat over the Internet!
   Kara Right. . . . I forgot about that!

2. Yumi Hi, Brad. How was your business trip?
   Brad To tell you the truth, it was awful. The day I left, the traffic was really bad, so I got to the airport late. And _____ I missed my flight.
   Yumi So, you were probably late for the sales meeting, then?
   Brad Yeah _____ . Then, because I was so stressed out, I forgot to give Mr. Yamamoto my business card.
   Yumi I'm sure he understood.
   Brad Yeah, and I apologized right away _____ .
   Yumi So, it doesn't sound like your trip was that bad.

4 About you 2

Conversation strategies **Answer the questions directly and confidently with true information. Then add a follow-up sentence with *of course*.**

1. Would you jump at the chance to study in another country?
   I'd absolutely jump at the chance to study in another country.
   Of course, I'd have to learn the language first.
2. What would you miss about your country if you lived abroad?
   _____
   _____
3. If you had the opportunity to live someplace else, where would it be?
   _____
   _____
4. What would be the first thing you'd do after moving to a new city?
   _____
   _____

1 Proverbs for everyday living

Reading **A Read the article. Which sentence best states the writer's attitude toward proverbs?**

1. Proverbs are fun but not meaningful.
2. Proverbs about love are truer than proverbs about sports or money.
3. Proverbs can help and guide us in different life situations.
4. Proverbs are never true.

Timeless wisdom

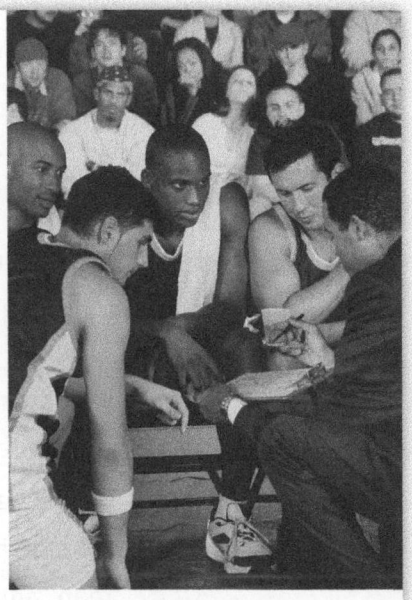

No matter what problem we have or what issue we are discussing, there always seems to be a memorable proverb that neatly sums up the situation, provides some wisdom, or simply makes us feel better. We find a selection that will inspire us, make us wiser, and console us through hard times. Sports, money, and love are just three of the areas that have inspired a number of well-used proverbs.

SPORTS There are probably few coaches who haven't called on a proverb or two to motivate their players. Players who aren't working to their full potential might benefit from hearing "no pain, no gain" and understand that increasing performance on the field requires more hard work and effort. During intense parts of a game, a coach might yell, "No guts, no glory!" to push his or her players into scoring a goal. "There is no *I* in *team*" encourages teamwork and reminds players that not being the "star" of the team might be hard, but it could mean a stronger winning team.

MONEY The proverb "A fool and his money are soon parted" describes a person who has money but squanders it on poor choices. A person who doesn't understand that it takes hard work to make money might benefit from the proverb "Money doesn't grow on trees." If it did, it would be easy to find and everyone would have an abundance of it. On the other hand, it's important to remember that money isn't always the answer to our problems. Sometimes we have to remind ourselves that "the best things in life are free" – for example, good health, family, and friends.

LOVE The proverb "Love is blind" means that if you are in love with someone, you overlook all their negative points. It's often said when you don't approve of a friend's partner; it offers an explanation for what you see as a poor choice. Then, when relationships go through sad or emotional times, the proverb "Love conquers all" reminds us that it's wise to approach these problems with love because they will be easier to handle. Love will get you through most difficult situations.

B Find these words and phrases in the article. Match them with their definitions.

1. sums up __f__
2. console ____
3. potential ____
4. squander ____
5. abundance ____
6. conquers ____

a. waste
b. ability
c. an amount that is more than enough
d. defeats, beats
e. give comfort or sympathy to
✓f. explains without detail

2 If at first you don't succeed, . . .

Writing **A Read about an athlete's favorite proverb. Fill in the blanks with the expressions in the box.**

I like this proverb because	it means that
it's often said that	one of my favorite proverbs is

As a college wrestler, I compete with some of the toughest and most disciplined athletes. _____ "fall seven times, stand up eight." To me, _____ you should never give up on your goals and dreams no matter how hard practice is every day or how many important matches you lose. _____ athletes can't win unless they believe in themselves. _____ it reminds me that no matter how many times I fail, if I don't stand up after my failure, I'll never succeed.

B Describe a proverb that you use for motivation in your life. Use the expressions above.

Unit 3 Progress chart

	What can you do? Mark the boxes. ✓ = I can . . . ? = I need to review how to . . .	To review, go back to these pages in the Student's Book.
Grammar	☐ use the simple present passive to talk about cultural traditions. ☐ use verb + *-ing* as a subject, and as an object of a preposition. ☐ use *to* + verb after *It's*.	22 and 23 24 and 25 24 and 25
Vocabulary	☐ use at least 10 expressions to talk about different customs and manners.	24 and 25
Conversation strategies	☐ use expressions like *to be honest* to sound more direct. ☐ use *of course* to give information that is not surprising or to agree.	26 27
Writing	☐ use expressions like *It means . . .* to talk about culture or proverbs.	29

Socializing

UNIT 4

Lesson A Party time

1 What are you supposed to do?

Grammar and vocabulary **Look at the pictures. Complete the sentences with *be supposed to* and an appropriate verb. Use negatives where necessary.**

1. You *'re not supposed to park* on the street.
   You *'re supposed to park* in the parking lot.

2. They _____ shoes inside.
   They _____ their shoes.

3. She _____ at the dentist.
   She _____ home.

4. He _____ his room.
   He _____ on the phone.

2 It was supposed to be a nice weekend.

Grammar **Complete the email with the correct form of *be supposed to* or *was / were going to*. Sometimes more than one answer is possible.**

New Message

Hey Jane,

I had a terrible weekend. On Saturday morning, I *was going to / was supposed to* go running with a friend because the weather _____ be nice. But it rained, and she didn't come. She emailed me and wrote, "I _____ come, but when I saw the weather, I decided to stay in bed. Sorry."

Then my parents came over to my apartment – they were two hours early. They _____ come at 1:00, but they came at 11:00. The apartment was a complete mess! They took me to that new Mexican place on Oak Street. Have you been there? It _____ be really good. But it was completely booked – I didn't realize that you _____ make reservations.

So then we tried an Italian place across the street. That was nice, but I didn't know my pasta dish had shrimp in it. I'm allergic to shrimp, and I _____ avoid it. So I got sick. Now here's the worst part. I _____ go to a party on Saturday night, but I couldn't because I still felt sick. I sure hope next weekend will be better.

Take care!
Allie

3 I was supposed to . . .

Grammar **Complete the conversation with the correct form of *be supposed to* or *was / were going to*. Sometimes more than one correct answer is possible.**

Christy Hi, Zach. Are you going to Isabelle's party tonight?

Zach Yeah, I am, actually. I *was supposed to meet / was going to meet* (meet) my parents for dinner, but they canceled. So, now I can go.

Christy Great! I _____ (pick up) Sanjay at 7:00. Do you need a ride?

Zach Sure, thanks. Now, I can't remember. . . . _____ we _____ (bring) anything like food or drinks?

Christy No, only if you want to. I _____ (not / make) anything, but maybe I will if I have time.

Zach You should make those chocolate chip cookies you brought to the last party. They were awesome.

Christy Yeah, they are pretty good. But they have nuts in them. Isabelle _____ (not / eat) nuts because she's allergic to them.

Zach Right. Maybe you should just make a chocolate cake or something.

Christy Good idea. Oh, and don't forget to bring your bathing suit and a towel. The weather _____ (be) great tonight, and Isabelle's pool is beautiful.

Zach Sounds like a plan to me!

4 About you

Grammar **Answer the questions with your own information. Use *be supposed to* or *was / were going to*. Use negatives and contractions where necessary.**

1. Is there anything you have to do to prepare for your English class?
   For our next class, we're supposed to bring in some photos.
2. What's the weather forecast for tomorrow?
   _____
3. What do you have to do tomorrow?
   _____
4. What plans do you have for this week?
   _____
5. What appointment or plans did you cancel last month?
   _____
6. What exciting future plans do you have?
   _____

Lesson B We have to get going.

1 Get away with . . .

Vocabulary **A Complete the sentences with the appropriate *get* expression.**

1. In some companies, you can _g_ _e_ _t_ _a_ _w_ _a_ _y_ _w_ _i_ _t_ _h_ wearing casual clothes to work. In my company, you have to dress more formally.
2. I'm so busy at work that I don't have time to answer all my emails right away, but I always ___ ___ ___ ___ ___ ___ ___ ___ ___ ___ ___ them eventually.
3. I have a business trip next week, but I'm going to try to ___ ___ ___ ___ ___ ___ ___ ___ it. I'm tired of traveling so much.
4. Someone else got the promotion I wanted at work. I'm upset, but I'll ___ ___ ___ ___ ___ ___ ___ ___ it soon.
5. My friend's always late for work. I just don't ___ ___ ___ ___ ___ ___ ! How does he keep his job?
6. My office doesn't have windows. It's depressing. I don't think I'll ever ___ ___ ___ ___ ___ ___ ___ ___ ___ not having sunlight.
7. During the summer, my company has new hours – we ___ ___ ___ ___ ___ ___ work at noon on Fridays!
8. My boss never returns my phone calls. I ___ ___ ___ ___ ___ ___ ___ ___ ___ ___ ___ ___ ___ that he's avoiding me.
9. Tonight there's a company party so new employees can ___ ___ ___ ___ ___ ___ ___ ___ ___ ___ everyone. I really hope to ___ ___ ___ ___ ___ ___ ___ ___ early. I hate these functions. But, the good food should help me ___ ___ ___ ___ ___ ___ ___ ___ ___ ___ ___ it OK.
10. I have a meeting in ten minutes! I really have to ___ ___ ___ ___ ___ ___ ___ ___ ___ .

B Complete the conversations with some of the *get* expressions from part A.

1. A Oh, I can't believe it's already 8:30! I'd better _get going_ if I want to catch the 9:00 train.
   B Yeah, I don't think you can _____ being late again.
   A I know, but it's so hard to get up in the morning. . . .
   B I don't _____ . How can you complain? You _____ work so early. I'd love your job!
2. A What time do you think you'll finish work tonight? Do you think you can _____ from work a little early?
   B Sure, I have a late meeting, but I can probably _____ it. Why? I _____ you have something planned. . . .
   A Did you _____ reading yesterday's restaurant review?
   B Yeah, for that amazing restaurant with the six-month waiting list?
   A Well, we're going tonight!

2 I get the feeling . . .

Grammar and vocabulary

Complete the anecdotes. Put the words in order and use the correct form of the verbs.

1. Melanie was very superstitious. She couldn't *get over her fear* (over / her fear / get) of seeing black cats. She thought they were so unlucky. Now she can't _____ (get / a day / through) without running into one.

2. Gary was supposed to meet Tracy at the movies, but he really wanted to _____ (get / of / go / out) with her. He called Tracy and said he couldn't _____ (work / off / get) early on Friday night. Instead, Gary made arrangements to go to the movies with Marissa. He really thought he could _____ (it / away / get / with). But he didn't – as he found out when he ran into Tracy at the movie theater!

3. John didn't _____ (pay / around / to / get) his electricity bill. He thought he could _____ (get / with / away / make) the payment a few days late. Now he has to _____ (to / used / eat / get) dinner in the dark!

3 About you

Grammar and vocabulary

Answer the questions with true information.

1. What haven't you gotten around to doing this week?
   I haven't gotten around to cleaning my room.
2. Have you bought anything new that took time to get used to?
   _____
3. What's a chore you always try to get out of doing?
   _____
4. What events do you find it hard to get through?
   _____
5. What time do you get off work?
   _____
6. How long did it take you to get over your last cold?
   _____

1 So, you're throwing a party?

Conversation strategies

A Unscramble these statement questions.

1. right / you, / is / It ?
   It is you, right?
2. teenagers, / huh / So / teach / you ?
   _____
3. them / haven't / So / told / you / yet ?
   _____
4. that software company, / working / still / You're / at / right ?
   _____
5. know / then / here, / don't / So / they / you're ?
   _____
6. huh / about / didn't / You / hear / that, ?
   _____

B Complete the conversation with the statement questions from part A.

Eva Oh, my gosh. Dan? I haven't seen you in ages!

Dan Eva? *It is you, right?* You look great! How are you?

Eva Oh, I'm fine. Thanks. So, what are you up to?
_____

Dan Cyber-trex? Actually, no, not anymore. They went out of business. _____

Eva No, I didn't. I'm sorry.

Dan Oh, it's OK. I'm at Micro-com now. I like it a lot better. So, what's up with you?

Eva Um, I teach history at the local high school.

Dan Wow! _____ What's that like?

Eva It's really good. The students are great. Anyway, what brings you back here?

Dan Well, I'm in town to throw my parents a surprise party for their 40th wedding anniversary.

Eva _____

Dan No, not yet! In fact, my brother and sister don't even know I'm here.

Eva _____ About the party, I mean.

Dan No, I couldn't. They can't keep a secret to save their lives!

2 So, you're having a birthday party?

Conversation strategies

Find three more places where you can use *so* in the conversation. Change the capital letters and add commas where necessary. Then write which meaning of *so* you are using: 1 = to start a topic with a question; 2 = to check your understanding; 3 = to pause or let the other person draw a conclusion; 4 = to close a topic.

Rita So, ~~Y~~you're having a birthday party this year? 1

Craig I don't know. ____ My birthday is going to fall right in the middle of final exams. ____

Rita ____ You think people won't come if they're studying? ____

Craig Yeah, I mean, these are important exams, _____ . . . you know, everyone is working hard to get good grades. ____

Rita ____ Well, maybe you could wait until after the exams are over. ____

Craig Yeah, I guess I could.

Rita Then you can have a double celebration: for your birthday *and* the end of exams. ____ ____

Craig That's a good idea.

Rita ____ Don't forget to invite me! ____

Craig I won't!

3 A late night

Conversation strategies

Complete the conversation with the sentences in the box.

So you're not too tired to go out tonight?	You're going out again tonight?
You didn't do anything?	✓You stayed out pretty late, huh?
You had a good time, right?	

Keith Oh, . . . I'm so tired. That was a long night last night.

Phil *You stayed out pretty late, huh?*

Keith Yeah, until about 2:30 in the morning. But it was fun.

Phil _____

Keith Oh, definitely. The band was great – just awesome. So, anyway, what about you? Did you go out?

Phil No. . . . I just stayed home. That's all.

Keith _____

Phil No. I was just here all night.

Keith Too bad. Do you want to come out tonight? Are you doing anything?

Phil I don't have any plans yet. _____

Keith Well, I was thinking about it. But I don't want to be out too late.

Phil _____

Keith Too tired to go out? No way! I'll be fine later.

Phil Sounds good to me.

1 First impressions

Reading **A Read the article. Then add the correct heading to each section.**

Be fearless. Pay attention to your body language. Use your ears.
Maintain eye contact. ✓Smile!

SOCIALIZING 101

Whether you are an extrovert or an introvert, one thing is certain: Almost everyone experiences some degree of stress when it comes to being sociable in new situations. It doesn't matter if you're starting a new job, going back to school, or if you're waiting in line at a coffee shop. The next time you're out and about, try one of these tips to help you become better at socializing.

Smile! One of the easiest and most effective ways to be more sociable is to smile. Remember: You're supposed to be having fun. When you strike up a conversation, a warm smile will make you seem more approachable and friendly. Don't be surprised when the person you start a conversation with reciprocates with an equally warm smile!

_____ Once you've started a conversation, make sure you keep your eyes focused on the person you're talking to. There's nothing more off-putting than talking to someone whose eyes are wandering around the room rather than paying attention to the conversation. Not every conversation is interesting, but there's no reason to be rude.

_____ When you cross your arms in front of you while standing or you cross your legs while sitting, you are literally keeping people at a distance. Try to keep an open, relaxed position, and people will feel more comfortable approaching you.

_____ Having a conversation is a two-way street. Ask engaging questions, and then really listen to what your conversation partner says. Who knows? You may discover you have common musical interests, or you might even get a recommendation for a great restaurant. You'll never know if you don't listen closely.

_____ Don't stand around waiting for someone to start talking with you. Get over your fear and be the person who initiates conversations. Most people are open to having a warm, meaningful conversation, especially when they are out in a social situation. Walking up to a stranger may seem daunting at first, but once you've done it a few times, it will seem natural and maybe even fun!

B Find these words and expressions in the article. Match them with their meanings.

1. reciprocate *e*
2. off-putting ____
3. wandering ____
4. literally ____
5. engaging ____
6. initiate ____
7. daunting ____

a. interesting
b. actually
c. slightly frightening
d. annoying or unpleasant
✓e. behave in the same way
f. going around with no clear purpose
g. start, cause something to begin

C Read the article again. Check (✓) the statements that the writer of the article would agree with. Cross (✗) the ones that the writer wouldn't agree with.

1. ✗ There's no reason to be nervous when you socialize.
2. ✓ Socializing is easier when you smile.
3. ____ People are supposed to enjoy socializing.
4. ____ It's not rude to look around the room when you're talking to someone.
5. ____ Crossing your arms is a good idea because it helps you feel comfortable.
6. ____ Socializing is more difficult when you only listen.
7. ____ Conversations with strangers can lead to all kinds of new possibilities.
8. ____ You can get used to socializing, and then it will be easier.

2 As an introvert

Writing **A Read the short article about meeting new people. Replace each underlined *as* with *because*, *being*, or *while*.**

As an introvert, I have a hard time meeting new people. I usually don't like to go to parties where there are lots of people I don't know.

When I travel, though, I am less shy. I find I can talk to people as I wait to get on a plane or train. Maybe I feel more comfortable as I'm away from home and I can be who I want to be. But when I get back home, I'm shy again!

B Write a short article about how you meet new people.

Unit 4 Progress chart

	What can you do? Mark the boxes. ✓ = I can . . . ? = I need to review how to . . .	To review, go back to these pages in the Student's Book.
Grammar	☐ use *be supposed to* to say what should happen.	34 and 35
	☐ use *be supposed to* to talk about things I should do.	34 and 35
	☐ use *was / were supposed to* and *was / were going to* for things that didn't happen.	34 and 35
	☐ use inseparable phrasal verbs with and without prepositions.	36 and 37
Vocabulary	☐ use at least 10 new expressions with *get*.	36 and 37
Conversation strategies	☐ use statement questions to check understanding.	38
	☐ use *so* to start or close topics, pause, or check understanding.	39
Writing	☐ use three different meanings of *as*.	41

Law and order

UNIT 5

Lesson A Rules and regulations

1 Something ought to be done.

Grammar **Rewrite the sentences in the passive form, starting with the words given.**

1. They must change the law. — The law *must be changed* .
2. They should ban fireworks. — Fireworks _____ .
3. They ought to fine people who litter. — People who litter _____ .
4. They shouldn't allow smoking on the street. — Smoking _____ on the street.
5. They could encourage healthy eating in schools. — Healthy eating _____ in schools.
6. They have to do something about violent movies. — Something _____ about violent movies.

2 What's your opinion?

Grammar and vocabulary **A Circle the correct words to complete the opinions.**

1. People should not be **encouraged** / **changed** / **passed** to keep dangerous pets like snakes and spiders.
2. Cell phones shouldn't be **fined** / **allowed** / **given** in museums.
3. People who litter should be **encouraged** / **allowed** / **fined** at least $100 for each item they drop.
4. People should be **given** / **made** / **changed** to vote.
5. Laws have to be **passed** / **arrested** / **done** to ban smoking in all public places.
6. Young people ought to be **banned** / **made** / **given** a driving test every year until they are 21.
7. Smoking on city streets could easily be **made** / **passed** / **banned**.
8. People should be **arrested** / **made** / **changed** for not carrying an ID.

B Do you agree or disagree with the opinions in part A? Answer with your own opinions.

1. *I agree completely. I don't think people should be allowed to keep dangerous pets at all.*
2. _____
3. _____
4. _____
5. _____
6. _____
7. _____
8. _____

3 What should be done?

Grammar **Read the situations and complete the comments. Use the passive of the verbs given.**

1. A woman is facing a large fine because her neighbor complained to the police about her messy yard. The angry woman then dumped her garbage in the neighbor's yard.
   A I think the fine is absolutely right. You shouldn't *be allowed* (allow) to have a messy yard.
   B I don't agree. She shouldn't _____ (fine). It's her own property, and she should be able to do what she wants.
   C The woman should _____ (arrest) for dumping garbage in her neighbor's yard!
2. A motorcycle rider was arrested by the police for refusing to wear a helmet. The motorcyclist said that he couldn't wear the helmet because of his traditional headdress.
   A I agree with the motorcyclist. He shouldn't _____ (make) to wear a helmet.
   B People shouldn't _____ (arrest) for not wearing a helmet. It's their choice.
   C Well, everyone has to obey the law. People shouldn't _____ (treat) differently.
3. A foreign exchange student who failed to show his ID was given a warning after a local storeowner called the police. In an unrelated incident, a young woman riding her bike to work was fined for failing to carry her ID.
   A I didn't know you could _____ (fine) for not carrying an ID.
   B It's a new law, but I think it ought to _____ (change).
   C I wonder why the police stopped the woman. People shouldn't _____ (stop) for no reason.

4 About you

Grammar **Read the situations and give your own opinion. Use passive modal verbs.**

1. A 13-year-old boy sneaks into an R-rated movie. What ought to be done?
   He ought to be made to tell his parents.
2. A man throws a soda can out of his car window. Should he be arrested or fined?
   _____
3. A 16-year-old student wants a part-time job. Should she be encouraged to get one?
   _____
4. A 15-year-old girl applies for a credit card. Should she be given one?
   _____
5. A 12-year-old boy spends three hours a day online. Should he be given a time limit?
   _____
6. An 85-year-old man was in six minor car accidents this year. Should he be allowed to drive?
   _____

Lesson B Crime and punishment

1 What's the crime?

Vocabulary **Match the words in Column A with the words in Column B to make expressions for crimes and punishments. Write the expressions under the appropriate heading in the chart.**

Column A	Column B
put	a house
armed	offense
lose	on probation
break into	robbery
kill	graffiti
take someone	to prison
send	captive
minor	jail
clean up	your license
go to	someone

Crime	Punishment
	put on probation

2 News flash

Vocabulary **Complete the news flashes with the words in the box.**

jaywalker	penalties	sentence	stealing
kidnapper	robbers	✓ shoplifters	vandals

1. *A TV actress was caught stealing in a designer store. The manager said* ___*shoplifters*___ *will be punished even if they're famous.*
2. *The number of robberies has declined. Police say more* _____ *are getting caught.*
3. *A murderer who was convicted of killing his boss receives a* _____ *of life in prison.*
4. *Three* _____ *were caught on camera spray-painting graffiti on office buildings. All three were put on probation for two years.*
5. _____ *for a first-time speeding offense now include a $500 fine.*
6. *A* _____ *was arrested after crossing in the middle of a busy street.*
7. *A* _____ *demands $10,000,000 after taking a politician's daughter from her home.*
8. *A teen was arrested for* _____ *money from a neighbor's house. Police say the 17-year-old broke into the neighbor's house while she was at work.*

3 In the news

Grammar **Imagine you are telling a friend about the excerpts from the newspaper below. Rewrite each sentence in the passive. Change the underlined verbs to the *get* passive, or use the *be* passive with *should*. Make any other necessary changes.**

1 Police arrested three teenagers yesterday for stealing a car. **2** The officers caught them joyriding along a busy street. **3** The owner of the car thinks they should fine the teens.

1. "*Three teenagers got arrested yesterday for stealing a car.*"
2. "_____"
3. "_____"

4 Fans think a TV network should make reality-TV star Lulu Maxwell give a public apology. **5** The county court fined Maxwell $500 and put her on probation for six months. **6** Store detectives caught her shoplifting in a department store downtown in March of this year.

4. "_____"
5. "_____"
6. "_____"

7 Car owners caught a man writing graffiti on their cars last Wednesday. **8** The judge convicted Jim Hillman yesterday of vandalism. **9** The owners of the cars believe they should make Hillman pay for the damage done to their vehicles.

7. "_____"
8. "_____"
9. "_____"

4 About you

Grammar **Answer the questions with true information. Use the *get* passive.**

1. What happens if you get caught shoplifting in your country?
   You get fined and perhaps put in jail.
2. What's the punishment for writing graffiti on a public building?
   _____
3. What's the punishment for murder?
   _____
4. What happens if you jaywalk?
   _____
5. What happens if you get caught speeding too many times?
   _____

1 Basically, I don't think . . .

Conversation strategies **Choose the best expressions to complete the conversation.**

Roy Did you know that Sam got caught cheating on the test?

Helen Yeah, it's about time. He cheats on all his tests. I wonder what the teacher's going to do about it.

Roy I don't know. What do you think they should do?

Helen Hmm. Well, **another thing is** / **basically,** I don't think he should get away with it.

Roy Well, no, I guess not.

Helen I mean, **for a couple of reasons** / **the point is**. First of all, it's not fair to the other students, and **number one** / **second of all**, it doesn't help the person who cheats. I mean, **the thing is** / **another thing is**, I don't think Sam's really learning.

Roy I know what you mean.

Helen And **for two reasons** / **another thing is**, if they don't punish him, it might make other students think they can cheat, too.

Roy Yeah. I guess you're right.

2 I mean, the thing is, . . .

Conversation strategies **A Read what Carl has to say about carrying ID cards. Number the lines in the correct order from 1 to 7.**

____ I mean, ID cards make things easier for two reasons.

__1__ What do I think about having to carry an ID card?

____ And then, secondly, if you have an accident or something, people can find out who you are right away.

____ And finally . . . um, I guess I just don't mind. You have nothing to be afraid of if you have nothing to hide. Don't you think?

____ First, they help the police identify criminals more easily.

____ Well, I guess basically, I'm in favor of carrying them.

____ And another thing is, people who work in movie theaters and other places can easily check who is old enough to go in and stuff.

B What do you think about carrying an ID card? Write four sentences. Use words and expressions from part A and Exercise 1 to organize your ideas.

_____

_____

_____

_____

_____

3 That's true, but . . .

Conversation strategies **Match Diego's opinions with his friends' responses. There is one extra response.**

1. I don't think jaywalking should be a crime. I mean, if I'm in a hurry, I should be able to cross the street wherever I want to! ____

2. I think couples that are getting married should be made to take marriage classes before they actually get married. You know, to help lower divorce rates. ____

3. I think it's the parents' responsibility to make sure their kids know right from wrong. I mean, if the kids do something wrong, their parents should be punished, too. ____

4. You know, there are just too many laws for everything! The thing is, most people are sensible enough not to need all these laws. ____

a. You've got a point there, but don't you think that parents with kids that are always in trouble should be helped, not punished?

b. Well, you've got a point, but society would be a big mess without them! I think people actually need them.

c. That's true – maybe it shouldn't be a crime – but you still need to be careful, especially if you're in a hurry.

d. That's true, but on the other hand, kids are kids, and we have to treat them all the same.

e. I never really thought of it that way. It's not such a bad idea, but I'm not sure that taking classes would help.

4 The point is, . . .

Conversation strategies **Complete the conversation with the words and expressions in the box.**

another thing is	I never thought of it that way	number two	there are two reasons
basically	number one	✓ their point is	you've got a point

Pam Did you hear they won't let students bring snacks to class anymore? Some teachers complained that students spend too much time eating when they should be taking notes. I guess *their point is*, students aren't paying enough attention.

Roger I don't think that's right. I mean, _____, you should be allowed to bring a snack.

Pam Why do you think that?

Roger Well, I mean, . . . _____. I guess, _____, you don't always have enough time between classes to get something to eat. And _____, some classes are three hours long! You really need to eat just to stay awake! And, _____, the teachers sometimes have drinks and things while they're teaching.

Pam Hmm. . . . _____ there, but in some classes, students just leave the garbage from their snacks and drinks all over the desks. It's really disgusting.

Roger Yeah, that's true. I must admit, . . . _____.

1 Dumb criminals

Reading **A** Read the article below. Then match the stories with the pictures.

Dumb Criminals

We all know that crime is serious and that criminals should be punished. However, it's hard not to smile when you hear about criminals like the ones in these stories, who made some dumb mistakes.

1. A thief stole 27 shoes from a store, without realizing that they were all right-footed. He wasn't arrested, but he certainly didn't get what he wanted.
2. A burglar was caught sleeping in an armchair of the house he was burglarizing when the owners came home.
3. Robbers stole $1,221 of electronics from a store. All the goods were faulty items returned by customers.
4. A man stole a police car in order to get to work. He was discovered when he stopped to help someone on the side of the road who flagged him down for help.
5. A woman walked into a fast-food restaurant early one morning and demanded money. The clerk said he couldn't open the cash drawer without a food order. When the woman grudgingly ordered onion rings, the clerk said they weren't available for breakfast. The woman became frustrated and walked out.
6. A man walked into a convenience store and asked for change, putting a twenty-dollar bill on the counter. When the cashier opened the drawer, the man demanded all the money in it. Then he ran out, leaving his twenty on the counter. The cashier reported that the man fled with about $17 in cash.

B Answer the questions about the criminals above.

Criminal 1: What didn't he notice? *He didn't notice all the shoes were right-footed.*

Criminal 2: Why was he caught? _____

Criminal 3: Why weren't these robbers happy? _____

Criminal 4: What was his mistake? _____

Criminal 5: What did she need to order? _____

Criminal 6: How much did his crime cost him? _____

2 A bad landing . . .

Writing **A** **Read the police report. Add *because*, *since*, or *as*. Sometimes more than one answer is possible.**

POLICE REPORT

A woman was arrested for trying to rob a convenience store. _____ she didn't know the store was open 24 hours a day, she broke in through the roof. Unfortunately for her, she fell through the roof and landed on top of a coffee machine. A police officer was inside the store, and he didn't have to go far to make the arrest _____ he was right there getting his coffee! _____ the woman was slightly injured, she went to the hospital first before going to jail. She was treated for minor cuts and coffee burns.

B **Write a short story or article about something funny that has happened to you. Use *because*, *since*, or *as* to give reasons for the events.**

Unit 5 Progress chart

	What can you do? Mark the boxes. ✓ = I can . . . ? = I need to review how to . . .	To review, go back to these pages in the Student's Book.
Grammar	☐ use the passive of modal verbs. ☐ use the *get* passive.	44 and 45 46 and 47
Vocabulary	☐ use at least 25 expressions to talk about rules, regulations, crimes, and punishments.	44, 45, 46, and 47
Conversation strategies	☐ organize what I say with expressions like *First of all*, etc. ☐ use expressions like *That's a good point* to show someone else has a valid argument.	48 49
Writing	☐ give reasons using *because*, *since*, and *as*.	51

Strange events

UNIT 6

Lesson A Coincidences

1 My strange experiences

Vocabulary **Complete Ava's blog with the words and expressions in the box.**

coincidences	out of the blue	sticks in my mind	✓UFO
déjà vu	ran into	telepathy	unexpectedly

Ava's Blog

Nothing really strange has ever happened to me. I've never seen a ___UFO___. And I don't believe in _____ – you know, that you can tell what someone else is thinking. I've never even had that strange feeling of _____, like I've been someplace before. The only weird thing that _____ is meeting someone with the same birthday as mine. But that's about it.

However, I absolutely believe strange _____ happen all the time. In fact, last week, I called a friend completely _____ at the same time she was calling me. That was pretty funny. A couple of years ago, I _____ that same friend at a restaurant while I was on vacation – completely _____. Oh, and another time, I was on the Internet and typed in the wrong URL. I found a website about my old high school science teacher. He'd invented a new type of vacuum cleaner and had become a millionaire! Cool, huh?

2 What a coincidence!

Grammar and vocabulary **Complete the story. Use the simple past or the past perfect. Sometimes more than one answer is possible.**

One night about a year ago, I went out with some friends. I didn't really want to go out because I ___had broken up___ (break up) with my girlfriend a week or so earlier. Anyway, I met this great girl, and we _____ (start) talking. We had a great time and danced all night. So, we _____ (decide) to meet the next day, and to make a long story short, we started dating.

We _____ (date) for about four months when she _____ (invite) me to a party at her apartment. I was looking at the pictures of her college friends around her apartment, and I _____ (notice) that my cousin Ciara from Chicago was in one of her photos. It turns out that my girlfriend and my cousin _____ (be) roommates for over three years in college, but they _____ (not see) each other for about a year. What a coincidence!

3 A mystery ride

Grammar and vocabulary **Read the story. Then answer the questions below using the past perfect.**

Last Tuesday, Peter got ready for his interview with a company called Compu-com. He left class and went to an ATM to get cash, but he didn't have time to get gas. He decided to get it early Wednesday morning. That night, he read over his cover letter and résumé. He felt confident. He always wrote good letters, and he had a great résumé with a nice photo. He had paid a professional to help him put it together.

Before going to bed, he got his things ready: his suit, shirt and tie, his best shoes. He set his alarm for 7:00 and went to sleep. But his cell phone was in silent mode, and he didn't hear it go off. Peter woke up at 8:30, but he left the house in two minutes flat! He didn't have enough gas to drive to Compu-com, so he decided to take a taxi. Of course, they were all occupied. After 15 minutes, a taxi stopped. There was a woman in the backseat. She asked, "Do you want a ride to Compu-com?" Peter didn't know her, but she obviously recognized him.

1. Why was Peter feeling confident? *He had written a good cover letter and résumé.*
2. Why was his résumé very strong? _____
3. Why did he sleep late on Wednesday morning? _____
4. Why was he able to leave home so quickly? _____
5. Why didn't he have enough gas to drive to the interview? _____
6. Why did he have enough money for a taxi? _____
7. Had Peter met the woman before? _____
8. How do you think the woman recognized Peter? _____

4 About you

Grammar **Write about a strange experience or coincidence that happened to you or someone you know. Use the simple past and past perfect. Use the ideas in the box or your own ideas.**

You received an email or a text from a friend you were thinking about.
You ran into an old friend on vacation in another part of your country.
You met someone with the same birthday as you.
You found an item that belonged to a friend in a strange place.
You gave a friend or family member the same present that he or she gave you.

_____

_____

_____

_____

_____

_____

1 Super superstitions

Vocabulary **What superstitions do these pictures illustrate? Write the superstition below each picture.**

1. *If you put your clothes on inside out, you'll get a nice surprise.*

2. _____

3. _____

4. _____

5. _____

6. _____

2 More world superstitions

Vocabulary **Complete the superstitions with the expressions in the box.**

broom	come into	come true	make	snake	sweep

1. Thailand: It's lucky to dream of a _____ because it means you'll meet the man or woman of your dreams.
2. China and Vietnam: It's bad luck to _____ the floor on New Year's Day with a _____. You'll take away your good fortune.
3. Turkey: If you stand between two people with the same name and _____ a wish, your wish will _____.
4. Ireland: If the palm of your right hand itches, it might mean you'll _____ money.

3 Are you superstitious?

Grammar **Complete the conversation with responses with *So* and *Neither*.**

Junya Are you superstitious?

Marta I'm not sure, actually.

Junya *Neither am I.*

Marta Do you believe in bad luck?

Junya Oh, do you mean like believing you'll have bad luck if you buy just one pillow? Well, I never buy just one.

Marta _____

Junya I mean, I don't believe it's unlucky. Still, I always buy two, just in case . . .

Marta _____ Anyway, why do you ask?

Junya Well, a friend of mine told me it's unlucky to sneeze only once.

Marta I didn't know that!

Junya _____ . . . But I *am* interested in all that stuff.

Marta _____ . . . So, does that mean we are superstitious, then?

4 I agree! . . . Or do I?

Grammar **Write two responses to each statement – one response with *So* or *Neither*, to show you are the same, and another showing you are different.**

1. I always make a wish when I see a falling star.

   So do I, if I see one.
   Really? I've never heard of that superstition.

2. I believe in telepathy.

   _____
   _____

3. I never cut my fingernails on Fridays.

   _____
   _____

4. I always pick up pennies for good luck.

   _____
   _____

5. I didn't know it was unlucky to spill salt.

   _____
   _____

Lesson C Weird and off the wall

1 Funny and hilarious

Conversation strategies **Choose the best word to repeat the underlined idea in each sentence.**

1. I have the funniest dreams, like one about me teaching a class in my robe and hair curlers. I mean, isn't that **frustrating** / **hilarious**?

2. I don't usually dream, so I find other people's dreams interesting to listen to. It's really **fascinating** / **scary** to listen to them.

3. I sometimes have this amazing dream that I can fly. It's just a **comical** / **wonderful** dream.

4. Every once in a while, I have this really scary dream. I'm driving along a road, and suddenly, I don't know how to drive! It's **disappointing** / **frightening**.

5. About once or twice a year, I have this strange dream that I'm back in college taking an important test. I mean, isn't it **weird** / **fascinating** to dream about something like that?

6. I wish I could remember my dreams, but it isn't easy. I mean, it's **difficult** / **important**. I heard you should write them down the moment you wake up.

2 How many ways can you say *beautiful*?

Conversation strategies **Complete each sentence by using a word to repeat the main idea in the first sentence.**

1. I often dream about a very attractive woman. She's really *beautiful*.
2. She's very easygoing. She's a really _____ kind of person.
3. She never gets annoyed. She never gets _____.
4. In my dream, we do some fun things together. You know, we do _____ stuff, like play games in the clouds.
5. They're always happy dreams. They're never _____.

3 Strong or soft

Conversation strategies **Read the comments. Does *just* make what the people say stronger or softer? Write *stronger* or *softer*.**

1. I didn't sleep well last night. I guess I just ate too much spicy food before I went to bed. *softer*
2. Last night, I dreamed I won ten million dollars! It was just the most incredible dream. _____
3. I don't really believe in superstitions. They're just a bit of fun. _____
4. I went to bed early last night. I was just exhausted. _____
5. I had a terrible nightmare last night. It was just the worst dream I've ever had. _____

4 About you

Conversation strategies **Write answers to the questions below. Use *just* to make your answers stronger or softer as necessary.**

1. Do you believe in telepathy? *Yes, I do. I think some people can really tell what others are thinking. It's just amazing.* **or** *No, I don't. I just don't believe you can ever tell what others are thinking.*
2. Do you like to watch TV shows about UFOs? _____
3. Do you think you can make something happen by wishing for it? _____
4. Do you believe that aliens exist? _____
5. Do you believe that dreams give us clues about our past or our future? _____

1 How strange is that?

Reading **A Read the stories. Write the number of the title that best describes each story.**

1. I Really, Really Love You!
2. Special Delivery . . . to Jail
3. Not a Book, but My Daughter
4. Reluctant Movie Star

Would You Believe . . . ?

WOULD YOU BELIEVE . . . ?

☐ Charles McLean, who works for a New York shipping company, wanted to visit his parents but didn't want to spend $320 on a plane ticket. Instead, he packed himself into a shipping crate and express-mailed himself to DeSoto, Texas. When the crate was delivered to his parents' home, he broke out of the box and shook hands with the delivery person. Unfortunately, the frightened woman did not have a sense of humor. She called the police, and McLean was arrested and charged as a stowaway.

☐ Julianne Clark, a makeup artist at a Hollywood movie studio, was working one Sunday afternoon. When she tried to drive home from the studio, she discovered that the exit gate was locked. As she tried to find another exit, she saw a bus full of people. She followed the bus, thinking it would lead her to an exit. But the bus was part of a movie. Clark followed the bus onto a ramp and slid into a large pool of water after the bus. No one was hurt, but it took security guards three hours to get her car out of the water!

☐ Christina Hudson of Denver, Colorado, is such a fan of Stephenie Meyer's *Twilight* books that she changed her name to include all four titles in the series. Hudson is now legally known as Christina Twilight New Moon Eclipse Breaking Dawn Hudson. Christina's mother and father don't mind that she changed her name to honor the *Twilight* books. They are just happy that she didn't choose to rename herself as a series of reality TV shows!

☐ Tim Wilson was worried about being late for his wedding when he crashed his car and broke his arm and leg. Refusing to stay in the hospital, he jumped into a taxi and arrived at the church just in time for the ceremony. But by the time he had cleaned himself up, his painkillers had worn off, and he passed out. He was rushed back to the hospital with his fiancée and the preacher, who married the couple as Wilson lay in his hospital bed.

B Read the article again and answer the questions. Then find words in the article to replace the underlined words.

1. Who couldn't find a way out (*an exit*) from her workplace? *Julianne Clark*
2. Who was the person that hid on a plane to avoid paying the fare? _____
3. Who took some medicine to stop pain, which then stopped working? _____
4. Who got into a large delivery box? _____
5. Who wanted to show her respect for a series of books? _____

2 Happily ever after . . .

Writing **A** **Read the story. Add *soon after, after,* or *before*.**

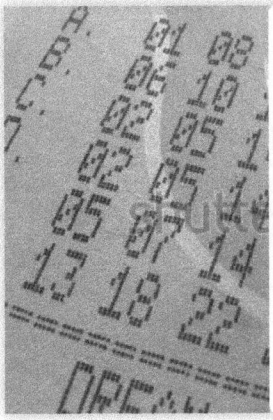

Steven Park and his wife Susan were having financial problems. One day, they each decided, without telling the other, to buy a lottery ticket. _____ buying these tickets, they had never spent money on the lottery. They both used numbers that were their anniversary date and address. That night, they were watching the news on TV, and the winning numbers were drawn. _____ hearing the familiar numbers, they started jumping up and down. They were shocked to find out that they each held a winning ticket! The Parks were $450,000 richer _____ picking up their winnings.

B **Write an amazing story you know, or make one up. Use prepositional time clauses.**

Unit 6 Progress chart

What can you do? Mark the boxes. ✓ = I can . . . ? = I need to review how to . . .	To review, go back to these pages in the Student's Book.
Grammar	
☐ use the past perfect.	54 and 55
☐ give responses with *So* and *Neither*.	57
Vocabulary	
☐ use at least 12 expressions to describe strange events and superstitions.	54, 55, and 56
Conversation strategies	
☐ make my meaning clear by repeating ideas.	58
☐ use *just* to make what I say stronger or softer.	59
Writing	
☐ use prepositional time clauses.	61

Illustration credits

Chuck Gonzales: 2, 3, 20, 21, 31, 44, 45, 54, 55, 94 **Frank Montagna:** 10, 11, 26, 27, 46, 47, 52, 67, 76, 78, 79 **Marilena Perilli:** 6, 7, 22, 23, 40, 58, 70, 71, 93 **Greg White:** 18, 38, 61, 69 **Terry Wong:** 12, 13, 28, 29, 50, 62, 63, 83, 90 **Q2A Studio Artists:** 59, 72

Photo credits

4 *(top to bottom)* ©Polka Dot Images/Thinkstock; ©Punchstock; ©Ryan McVay/Thinkstock **5** ©newphotoservice/Shutterstock **8** ©RON EDMONDS/Associated Press **14** ©Getty Images **15** ©Punchstock **16** *(left to right)* ©Mel Curtis/Getty Images/RF; ©Tim Garcha/Corbis; ©Kaz Chiba/Getty Images **18** © Tongro Image Stock/agefotostoc **19** *(top to bottom)* ©Tim Thompson/Corbis; ©David Lyons/Alamy; ©Watt, Elizabeth/agefotostock *(background)* ©Malchev/Shutterstock **24** ©Jim Arbogast/Getty Images/RF **30** ©Zero Creatives/Getty Images **31** ©Westend61/Getty Images/RF **32** ©Ryan McVay/Thinkstock **34** ©Punchstock **42** ©SnowWhiteimages/Shutterstock **49** ©Sean Gladwell/Shutterstock **60** *(top to bottom)* ©Andresr/Shutterstock; ©arek_malang/Shutterstock; © Ocean/Corbis/RF; © photomak/Shutterstock **64** ©ColinCramm/Shutterstock **66** ©SuperStock/agefotostock **67** ©George Doyle/Thinkstock **72** *(books)* ©LanKS/Shutterstock **74** *(top to bottom)* ©Kevork Djansezian/Getty Images; ©Thinkstock/Getty Images; ©PhotoAlto/James Hardy **75** *(top to bottom)* ©Kike Calvo/National Geographic Society/Corbis; ©Lane Oatey/Blue Jean Images/Getty Images/RF; ©Digital Vision/Getty Images; ©Punchstock; ©Wayne Eardley/Masterfile **77** *(top, top to bottom)* ©s_bukley/Shutterstock; ©Helga Esteb/Shutterstock *(bottom, left to right)* ©MGM/courtesy Everett Collection; ©MGM/courtesy Everett Collection; ©20th Century Fox Film Corp/Everett Collection; ©Alexandra Wyman/Getty Images **80** *(left to right)* ©D Dipasupil/FilmMagic/Getty Images; ©Jason LaVeris/FilmMagic/Getty Images *(diamond)* ©pdesign/Shutterstock *(background)* ©Ezepov Dmitry/Shutterstock **85** ©Sue Wilson/Alamy **86** ©Randy Faris/Corbis

Text credits

While every effort has been made, it has not always been possible to identify the sources of all the material used, or to trace all copyright holders. If any omissions are brought to our notice, we will be happy to include the appropriate acknowledgements on reprinting.

The top 500 spoken words

This is a list of the top 500 words in spoken North American English. It is based on a sample of four and a half million words of conversation from the Cambridge International Corpus. The most frequent word, *I*, is at the top of the list.

1. I
2. and
3. the
4. you
5. uh
6. to
7. a
8. that
9. it
10. of
11. yeah
12. know
13. in
14. like
15. they
16. have
17. so
18. was
19. but
20. is
21. it's
22. we
23. huh
24. just
25. oh
26. do
27. don't
28. that's
29. well
30. for
31. what
32. on
33. think
34. right
35. not
36. um
37. or
38. my
39. be
40. really
41. with
42. he
43. one
44. are
45. this
46. there
47. I'm
48. all
49. if
50. no
51. get
52. about
53. at
54. out
55. had
56. then
57. because
58. go
59. up
60. she
61. when
62. them
63. can
64. would
65. as
66. me
67. mean
68. some
69. good
70. got
71. OK
72. people
73. now
74. going
75. were
76. lot
77. your
78. time
79. see
80. how
81. they're
82. kind
83. here
84. from
85. did
86. something
87. too
88. more
89. very
90. want
91. little
92. been
93. things
94. an
95. you're
96. said
97. there's
98. I've
99. much
100. where
101. two
102. thing
103. her
104. didn't
105. other
106. say
107. back
108. could
109. their
110. our
111. guess
112. yes
113. way
114. has
115. down
116. we're
117. any

118. he's
119. work
120. take
121. even
122. those
123. over
124. probably
125. him
126. who
127. put
128. years
129. sure
130. can't
131. pretty
132. gonna
133. stuff
134. come
135. these
136. by
137. into
138. went
139. make
140. than
141. year
142. three
143. which
144. home
145. will
146. nice
147. never
148. only
149. his
150. doing
151. cause
152. off
153. I'll
154. maybe
155. real
156. why
157. big
158. actually
159. she's
160. day
161. five
162. always
163. school
164. look
165. still
166. around
167. anything
168. kids
169. first
170. does
171. need
172. us
173. should
174. talking
175. last
176. thought
177. doesn't
178. different
179. money
180. long
181. used
182. getting
183. same
184. four
185. every
186. new
187. everything
188. many
189. before
190. though
191. most
192. tell
193. being
194. bit
195. house
196. also
197. use
198. through
199. feel
200. course
201. what's
202. old
203. done
204. sort
205. great
206. bad
207. we've
208. another
209. car
210. true
211. whole
212. whatever
213. twenty
214. after
215. ever
216. find
217. care
218. better
219. hard
220. haven't
221. trying
222. give
223. I'd
224. problem
225. else
226. remember
227. might
228. again
229. pay
230. try
231. place
232. part
233. let
234. keep
235. children
236. anyway
237. came
238. six
239. family
240. wasn't
241. talk
242. made
243. hundred
244. night
245. call
246. saying

247. dollars
248. live
249. away
250. either
251. read
252. having
253. far
254. watch
255. week
256. mhm
257. quite
258. enough
259. next
260. couple
261. own
262. wouldn't
263. ten
264. interesting
265. am
266. sometimes
267. bye
268. seems
269. heard
270. goes
271. called
272. point
273. ago
274. while
275. fact
276. once
277. seen
278. wanted
279. isn't
280. start
281. high
282. somebody
283. let's
284. times
285. guy
286. area
287. fun
288. they've
289. you've
290. started
291. job
292. says
293. play
294. usually
295. wow
296. exactly
297. took
298. few
299. child
300. thirty
301. buy
302. person
303. working
304. half
305. looking
306. someone
307. coming
308. eight
309. love
310. everybody
311. able
312. we'll
313. life
314. may
315. both
316. type
317. end
318. least
319. told
320. saw
321. college
322. ones
323. almost
324. since
325. days
326. couldn't
327. gets
328. guys
329. god
330. country
331. wait
332. yet
333. believe
334. thinking
335. funny
336. state
337. until
338. husband
339. idea
340. name
341. seven
342. together
343. each
344. hear
345. help
346. nothing
347. parents
348. room
349. today
350. makes
351. stay
352. mom
353. sounds
354. change
355. understand
356. such
357. gone
358. system
359. comes
360. thank
361. show
362. thousand
363. left
364. friends
365. class
366. already
367. eat
368. small
369. boy
370. paper
371. world
372. best
373. water
374. myself
375. run

376. they'll
377. won't
378. movie
379. cool
380. news
381. number
382. man
383. basically
384. nine
385. enjoy
386. bought
387. whether
388. especially
389. taking
390. sit
391. book
392. fifty
393. months
394. women
395. month
396. found
397. side
398. food
399. looks
400. summer
401. hmm
402. fine
403. hey
404. student
405. agree
406. mother
407. problems
408. city
409. second
410. definitely
411. spend
412. happened
413. hours
414. war
415. matter
416. supposed
417. worked
418. company
419. friend
420. set
421. minutes
422. morning
423. between
424. music
425. close
426. leave
427. wife
428. knew
429. pick
430. important
431. ask
432. hour
433. deal
434. mine
435. reason
436. credit
437. dog
438. group
439. turn
440. making
441. American
442. weeks
443. certain
444. less
445. must
446. dad
447. during
448. lived
449. forty
450. air
451. government
452. eighty
453. wonderful
454. seem
455. wrong
456. young
457. places
458. girl
459. happen
460. sorry
461. living
462. drive
463. outside
464. bring
465. easy
466. stop
467. percent
468. hand
469. gosh
470. top
471. cut
472. computer
473. tried
474. gotten
475. mind
476. business
477. anybody
478. takes
479. aren't
480. question
481. rather
482. twelve
483. phone
484. program
485. without
486. moved
487. gave
488. yep
489. case
490. looked
491. certainly
492. talked
493. beautiful
494. card
495. walk
496. married
497. anymore
498. you'll
499. middle
500. tax